HOW TO BECOME

FABULOUSLY WEALTHY

HOW TO BECOME
FABULOUSLY WEALTHY
AT HOME
IN 30 MINUTES

BY LETTING GO
OF THE DESIRE
TO BE WEALTHY

(the Bodhisattva Strategy)

Paul Williams

謙

Entwhistle Books

Entwhistle Books
P. O. Box 232517
Encinitas CA 92023
USA

ISBN: 0-934558-22-1

Electronic publishing and design
assistance: Jeff Schalles

Thanks to Thich Nhat Hanh, Pema Chödrön,
Kurt Vonnegut, Stephen Mitchell, Emmet Fox,
Richard Wilhelm, R.H. Blyth, Carol Anthony and
their publishers for the quotes from their
writings excerpted herein

the text of this booklet can also be found at:
www.wealthbook.com

to order more copies: send $7.95 + $2 shipping for one,
or $6.00 each for five or more copies + $4 total shipping
to above address or fax or phone: 760-753-1815

"ALL THINGS COME to the man who is modest and kind in a high position," according to the 5000-year-old Chinese book-oracle called the *I Ching*, Richard Wilhelm translation, page 60.

First of all, if you're a woman, retranslate this to read "all things come to the *woman* who is modest and kind in a high position."

Secondly, notice if your first thought is something like, "This doesn't apply to me, 'cause I'm not in a high position." Are you sure?? My friend, the simple fact that you're reading these words in English (if you are) and that you have obtained this pamphlet via "Internet shopping" or have found it in the sort of bookstore that would carry such a pamphlet, is reasonable evidence that you are among the relatively privileged and wealthy of the Earth at this historical moment. And if your historical moment is anytime close to mine (late '98 as I write this), you can consider yourself to be in a high position just to be alive and conscious and participating at this moment in human (or sentient biosphere) history.

OK, so if you will grant me that, looked at a certain way, you are indeed in a high position (also please consider how much the people closest to you, parents, children, siblings, lovers, friends, treasure you and depend on your presence and goodwill)... If you'll contemplate for a moment the ways in which you are in fact a man or woman in a high position, then what's left is to be modest and kind, to yourself, to dear ones, to strangers...

More on this further on, although I'm certain that every one of us already has some vague awareness of opportunities in our personal lives and everyday circumstances to be more modest (i.e., less certain of the Importance of what we're doing) and more kind.

So that's it, you've got the formula. *Be modest and kind.*

A further recipe, which in fact works reliably to make it easier to be modest and kind, is: *Count your blessings.* Almost everyone knows this wonderful tool. But since it's at least as useful as a crescent wrench or a mousepad, more details of how and when to do this exercise will be offered herein somewhere.

And then, glancing back at the title for a moment, the reader might reasonably expect some "how-to" tips regarding letting go and, specifically, letting go of the desire to be wealthy... Easier said than done, right? Yes, you're right. But I hope to include herein some succinct recipes from ancient sages regarding how this always-difficult process of letting go of strong feelings, in this case feelings of desire for something we imagine to be "wealth," can be successfully accomplished. At home. In less time than it takes to watch a TV program or to get online and answer four emails.

And yes, you can tell that impatient beast in you to relax and be assured that I am gonna provide some detail as to what I (or you) might mean by "fabulously wealthy" and how I (and the sages) can be so sure that you'll be pleased by the results and won't return our booklet demanding a full refund and a public apology....

Therefore, ladies & gentlemen, the

TABLE OF CONTENTS:

What Is Modesty?

THE STATEMENT "All things come to the man who is modest and kind in a high position" occurs in a chapter of the *I Ching* called "Possession in Great Measure," and there is a footnote attached to the statement in which Richard Wilhelm, who had served as a Protestant minister before beginning his translation of the ancient book, observes, "the meaning of this hexagram [the book is divided into chapters marked by six-line pictographs called hexagrams] parallels the saying of Jesus: 'Blessed are the meek; for they shall inherit the earth'."

To me there is another one of the Beatitudes, the eight blessings spoken by Jesus Christ at the beginning of his Sermon on the Mount (*Matthew* 5), that is an even closer parallel to the *I Ching*'s promise of possession in great measure to the person who is "modest and kind in a high position": "Blessed are the poor in spirit; for theirs is the kingdom of heaven."

"Blessed are the poor in spirit..."

The Christian essayist Emmet Fox, whose books were extremely popular in the United States in the 1930s, wrote about this Beatitude: "To be *poor in spirit* means to have emptied yourself of all desire to exercise personal self-will, and, what is just as important, to have renounced all preconceived opinions in the whole-hearted search for God. It means to be willing to set aside your present habits of thought, your present views and prejudices..."

That sounds like modesty to me.

This pamphlet's assertion that it is possible for the reader to become fabulously wealthy in thirty minutes is based on its author's enthusiasm upon hearing Confucius's wonderful promise, "All things come to the man who is modest and kind in a high position," and recognizing it as being very close to similar statements by Jesus Christ and the Buddha. If all these sages concur, surely this recipe is worth testing in our own lives, in a straightforward practical manner that may or may not have much to do with what you or I think of as "religion."

What did the Buddha say? Well, as with Jesus and Emmet Fox, and the ancient Chinese sages and Richard Wilhelm, I find it helpful to have a local (20th century) guide to the old teachings, so I turn to the translations of a Vietnamese monk named Thich Nhat Hanh, who offers this contemporary wording of a 2000-year-old Buddhist invocation of the bodhisattva or awakened being named Samantabhadra:

"We invoke your name, Samantabhadra. We aspire to practice your vow to act with the eyes and heart of compassion; to bring joy to one person in the morning and to ease the pain of one person in the afternoon. We know that the happiness of others is our own happiness. We know that if we practice wholeheartedly, we ourselves may become an inexhaustible source of peace and joy for our loved ones and for all species."

"But what about wealth?" you ask? Um, being an inexhaustible source of peace and joy for my loved ones and everyone else sounds about as close to the kingdom of heaven as I can personally visualize. But Emmet Fox acknowledges that the words "Blessed are the meek; for they shall inherit the earth" "seem to be obviously contradicted by the plain facts of everyday life." If the meek are the poor-in-material-goods people of our era or any era, then, we all would agree, the promise doesn't seem to have been kept. They own almost nothing, so how could they have inherited the earth? (The cynic comments that they seem to have inherited only the right to work the earth long hours with pick and plow on behalf of absentee owners.)

Let's switch again from the meek to the poor in spirit, because "theirs is the kingdom of heaven" somehow does sound like fabulous wealth to me. And Emmet Fox's interpretation of "poor in spirit" three pages back sounds quite compatible with what the *I Ching* has to say about modesty:

"When a person holds a high position and is nevertheless modest, he [she] shines with the light of wisdom. If he is in a lowly position and is modest, he cannot be passed by. The unassuming attitude of mind that goes with modesty fits a person to accomplish even difficult undertakings: he imposes no demands or stipulations but settles matters easily and quickly. [see chapter 2, What Is Kindness?]. Where no claims are put forward, no resistances arise."

"Where no claims are put forward, no resistances arise."

Dear reader, do resistances arise when I/we seem to be suggesting that putting no claims forward (and setting aside present views and prejudices) can result in fabulous wealth? How about if we just say that they can result in becoming an inexhaustible source of peace and joy for our loved ones and for all species?

How to be modest: Notice yourself thinking, a little impatiently, that it's very *important* that you get to work on time today, or that your friend understand what you just said, or when something else genuinely does seem important And when you notice this familiar thought, don't criticize it, don't defend it, just smile — with amusement and kindness — to yourself and to the others, human or inanimate, who seem to be obstacles to your immediate (and very important) progress. At this moment, gently empty yourself of the urgency of this moment. This is modesty. It gets easier with practice. "Breathing in, I forgive my wife/my husband/the other driver/my computer. Breathing out, I forgive myself, and smile."

What Is Kindness?

KINDNESS IS THE decision to be gentle, in speech and action, towards another person and towards oneself. Criticism and self-criticism are seldom kind...but gentle self-criticism can be, and very gentle and loving criticism of another can be kind, if done carefully, mindfully. Kindness is the expression, in one's communications and other actions, and in one's thoughts, of genuine compassion...which is the ability to perceive another's suffering as though it were one's own, and therefore to treat others as considerately and sympathetically as one wishes to be treated oneself.

Kindness is gentle, but not passive. It is an energetic practice of generosity towards the world, and even towards one's own mind and heart and self. "All things come to the person who is modest and kind," because he or she does not scare them away. The poor in spirit are blessed with the kingdom of heaven because their open modesty and simple kindness create such a kingdom all around them, and their reward is they get to live in it. Moment to moment.

"The happiness of others is our own happiness." To be a bodhisattva is to live as though the happiness of others matters. Christ, Buddha and Confucius all agree: this can bring immediate wealth.

When we are not kind to ourselves, it is difficult to be truly kind to others. Pema Chödrön, an American Buddhist nun in a Tibetan tradition, says, in her book *Awakening Loving-Kindness:*

"When people start to meditate or to work with any kind of spiritual discipline, they often think that somehow they're going to improve, which is a sort of subtle aggression against who they really are. Loving-kindness toward ourselves doesn't mean getting rid of anything. *Maitri* ["loving-kindness" in Sanskrit, a language of India in Buddha's era] means that we can still be crazy after all these years. We can still be angry after all these years. We can still be timid or jealous or full of feelings of unworthiness. The point is not to try to change ourselves. Meditation practice isn't about trying to throw ourselves away and become something better. It's about befriending who we are already."

I like it that Pema Chödrön, in the course of sharing the Buddha's 2500-year-old teachings, alludes to the words of a popular song by a contemporary singer-songwriter (Paul Simon, "Still Crazy After All These Years"). Along those lines, here is a quotation from Kurt Vonnegut, Jr.'s 1965 novel *God Bless You, Mr. Rosewater:*

[The protagonist, Eliot Rosewater, arguably the greatest fool figure in an American novel of the 20th century, is explaining to his estranged wife that a neighbor has insisted he baptize her twin children.]

"What will you say? [she asks] What will you do?"

"Oh — I don't know... Go over to her shack, I guess. Sprinkle some water on the babies, say, 'Hello, babies. Welcome to Earth. It's hot in the summer and cold in the winter. It's round and wet and crowded. At the outside, babies, you've got about a hundred years here. There's only one rule that I know of, babies — :

'God damn it, you've got to be kind'."

Counting Our Blessings

THE MEANING OF the phrase "count your blessings", considered as a simple (everyday) spiritual exercise, is:

Remind yourself, by making a mental list, of a few of the many ways in which you are fortunate, lucky, right now, today. "I live in or near a beautiful place." "I have good friends." "I am not in great physical pain now." "I am able to obtain — and enjoy — food and water when I need them."

Sometimes the exercise is referred to as, "count your blessings and not your sorrows." The point, of course, is that we have a choice of where we put our attention, and indeed if we're not attentive to where we focus our thoughts we may find ourselves almost compulsively creating or prolonging our own suffering. Dwelling, for example, on all the very good reasons I should stay angry or fearful right now, even though feeling anger or fear is an unpleasant experience. "Let me count the reasons!" Why don't you count the reasons to feel happy right now instead of the reasons to feel awful?

"Counting our blessings" is not just a matter of thinking positively or optimistically. What makes it such a powerful exercise is that we are in fact by our nature constantly taking an inventory of our circumstances. When we consciously play the little game called "counting my blessings," we directly and easily transform the reality we live in or anyway our perception of it and the way we feel about it. Plato said men cling to their own chains. Similarly, men and women cling to their own misery and depression and discomfort. We don't have to. Really, "counting your blessings," practiced as a sincere and frequent conscious exercise, is a cheap, quick, and universally available map to buried treasure. Fabulous wealth. No self-deception is involved. Quite the opposite. When we practice this little exercise sincerely, we *un*deceive ourselves. Not that we're ignoring or denying the bad news. But what a difference when we stay in touch with all the good news at the same time!

So here's how to "count your blessings":

Challenge yourself, when you have a moment for contemplation, to come up with an arbitrary number of "blessings" that you currently perceive in your own life. Three or four examples, say, or twelve. Don't be sloppy. Come up with three or four that really are blessings, unmistakably; things that actually do make you smile when you remind yourself of them. No one's listening but you, so don't try to fake it. Be rigorous in your self-honesty. Come up with a few identifiable "blessings" that, when you look at them this way, you really are grateful for.

Then try it again tomorrow. Try it when you're in a crummy mood as well as when you're in a good mood. The more you do this, the more easily and naturally it will come. Soon in the midst of depressing or aggravating or fear-provoking circumstances you'll find yourself spontaneously noticing blessings ("I'm really grateful I didn't drop that on my foot!" "Good that I wasn't so critical of myself this time!"). Practice often, and sincerely (with rigorous self-honesty), and you *will* feel blessed, and much more able to be modest and kind. Bodhisattvas aren't "do-gooders." They're genuinely happy (awakened) beings.

Thich Nhat Hanh (in his book *Peace Is Every Step*):

"The secret to happiness is happiness itself. Life is filled with many wonders, like the blue sky, the sunshine, the eyes of a baby. Our breathing, for example, can be very enjoyable. I enjoy breathing every day. But many people appreciate the joy of breathing only when they have asthma or a stuffed-up nose. We don't need to wait until we have asthma to enjoy our breathing. Awareness of the precious elements of happiness is itself the practice of right mindfulness. Elements like these are within us and all around us. In each second of our lives we can enjoy them. If we do so, seeds of peace, joy and happiness will be planted in us, and they will become strong."

Pema Chödrön (again from *Awakening Loving-Kindness*):

"Being satisfied with what we already have is a magical golden key to being alive in a full, unrestricted, and inspired way. It is just as if we had looked around to find out what would be the greatest wealth that we could possibly possess in order to lead a decent, good, completely fulfilling, energetic, inspired life, and found it all right here."

Letting Go

LETTING GO MEANS not holding on. When Plato said we cling to our own chains, he meant we imprison ourselves by holding on tight to ideas and feelings that wouldn't restrict us if we weren't so firmly attached to them via our own willful clinging.

No lock on our chains except the fierce grip of our own (mental) fingers.

Letting go of desire is like letting go of anger or terror or any powerful feeling. It isn't easy. But it can be done if you decide ahead of time that you are free to (can allow yourself to) release your attachment if and when the impulse strikes you.

"Let go!" That doesn't mean, "destroy the feeling of desire!" It just means, stop holding on to it so tightly. It'll come back of its own accord (and that's okay too). You don't have to be so attached to it. You'll be happier not being so attached to it. It will still be there but it won't make you jump every time it twitches.

Let go of specific desires (like the desire to be wealthy) by setting them (and yourself) free. Acknowledge their existence, but don't keep feeding them attention. That gives them power to blind you. Say hello, then look the other way, and see what happens. "This desire is not me. I have no need to be caught by it."

The title of this booklet is only partly a joke. The author really does believe great wealth can be achieved in thirty minutes, because the kind of wealth he's thinking of [see chapter 5, What Is Wealth?] is not the sort of far-off and ultimately disappointing fantasy that we're supposed to work for and struggle towards for decades, but rather something authentic and actual, a wealth that exists in the present moment, here and now.

In the Buddha's view (and perhaps Christ's and Confucius's and Plato's as well) great wealth is achieved (arrived at, recognized) by awakening. Letting go helps this process, of course. But one of the many things that needs to be let go of is the notion that it couldn't be a true awakening if it happened so quickly!

In the *Mumonkan,* a collection of classic Zen stories assembled in 1228 A.D., a monk asks his teacher to explain why Daitsu Chisho Buddha sat in meditation for ten million years yet didn't achieve enlightenment. Modern Zen student R. H. Blyth (a British prisoner of war in Japan in the 1940s) comments, "Psychologically speaking, it was Daitsu Chisho's desire for enlightenment that prevented him from getting it during an eternity of time. It was also this that blinded the monk and made him ask the question."

See how long it can take when you don't let go of the desire?

Conversely, the nice thing about spiritual awakening is you can get there in just a moment. And um, you can achieve this freedom (liberation) and fabulous wealth (the kingdom of heaven) again every time you success-fully set aside your present habits of thought (as Emmet Fox told us Jesus told us) and views and prejudices. Set aside = let go. Not a drastic act. But the results can be spectacular. Okay, when you do this in 30 minutes you can't nec-essarily stay there (in that awareness-of-fabulous-wealth) forever. But Buddha does reassure us (in his sutra on "The Four Establishments of Mindfulness") that after you've gotten there in 30 min-utes a number of times, you'll probably start being able to do it in 30 seconds. Hey, you can't get down to the local branch of the Bank of Mammon and roll in your money that fast!

What Is Wealth?

"I DON'T CARE too much for money, money can't buy me love." The Beatles may not be ancient sages (or they might be!), but it would not be difficult to find passages of Christian or Buddhist or Muslim or Taoist scripture supporting their basic argument here — that money can't buy (and therefore can't be equated with) happiness or peace of mind or true love.

What is wealth? The part of me and you that desires wealth tends to believe, rather stubbornly, that it's large amounts of money (enough currency to roll around in). When we think of wealthy people, we think of mansions (and so do they, of course). So that part of our minds may sincerely believe this booklet's title is a fraud if the reader isn't magically able to "buy" a mansion after a half hour of reading.

But the ancient sages teach that another part of our minds is always able to clear away confusion and delusion and in a moment's time suddenly recognize itself or its person as actually living in a splendid and wondrous mansion right now. With this kind of wealth you don't just "own" the mansion according to a piece of paper; you actually see it and touch it and experience it palpably as your safe and loving and proper home and environment. Your kingdom. Wealth beyond dreams of avarice (and thank goodness; life is much pleasanter when we get past those dreams).

Wealth is our inheritance — these bodies, this ocean, this sky, the eyes of children, music and paintings and theater and the ability to enjoy these art forms, friendship, sex, love and language and science and other man-made and natural wonders...

Wealth is the richness of our lives and opportunities and experiences here and now, on this planet.

You want to become fabulously wealthy? Open your eyes and your heart. You already are.

And all this wealth is yours to keep...but the catch is, you are not a separate self, you are all of us. "More wealthy" is not a meaningful concept. You can be, you already are, extraordinarily wealthy. And you can enjoy this wealth up to your personal limits for joy. On and on.

But if your real desire is not to be wealthy but to be more wealthy than others — I'm sorry, you can't have that except by deluding yourself. And the catch here is that it's only by *un*deluding ourselves that we can experience and enjoy our wealth.

Indeed you may find, like other bodhisattvas before you, that your greatest satisfaction and joy comes from giving to others. Sharing the wealth, literally. All things come to the person who is modest and kind because things only come to us because they want to be given away. That's their satisfaction and joy. Wealth is not actually *having* things. Wealth is letting stuff flow through us. Our inheritance. And our purpose here is to pass it along.

What is wealth? Wealth is what the *I Ching* calls "possession in great measure," what Christ calls "the kingdom of heaven," what Thich Nhat Hanh (speaking for the Buddha) calls "awareness of the precious elements of happiness."

Wealth is personal — something more immediate and tangible than a spot on a list of "the richest men in the world."

Wealth is awareness. Wealth is the ability to enjoy wondrous possessions, without fear or envy or regret. Wealth is visible abundance and the ability to accept and delight in (and see, smell, touch, recognize) this abundance. Yes, it can be lost — because, as the sages remind us, all things are subject to change — but the real test of wealth is whether it can be found, here and now.

To become fabulously wealthy we need to count our blessings, to be able to enjoy and accept what we have. Many who appear wealthy have difficulty with this part of the practice. Yet we envy them. Some confused part of our minds puts appearance above experience. Wealth is not appearance. Wealth is the actual, immediate enjoyment of the kingdom of heaven. Welcome. Please be modest and kind now that you've arrived.

What Is Desire?

IF THE STRATEGY for awakening to (and thereby gaining) the great wealth we already have involves letting go of the desire to be wealthy, we need to know what desire is, so we can recognize it and observe ourselves in the act of clinging to it. Will it be safe to let go of this? And which muscles or what sort of grip do I release?

Carol K. Anthony in her 1980 book of commentaries on the *I Ching* says: "Desire is a form of fear that we may not achieve our goal. We hardly ever desire what we are sure of having, and often desire what we think we cannot have. Thus, desire contains both doubt and envy. In letting go of these negative feelings we bring the heart to rest and attain a higher level of tranquility." Richard Wilhelm suggests that the words of the hexagram Anthony is discussing, "Keeping Still," "possibly embody directions for the practice of yoga." Anthony adds: "often receiving this hexagram is a call to meditate, or at least to get in touch with our [hidden] worries and fears."

The desire to "be" something is a longing or craving. Handling cravings successfully is a neverending challenge for us human critters.

Another one of the Beatitudes from the Sermon on the Mount reminds us that it is incorrect to think that desire and craving always have evil or destructive consequences. Jesus said, "Blessed are they which do hunger and thirst after righteousness [right thought, opportunities to practice modesty and kindness]; for they shall be filled."

Okay, so here's the riddle: why was his desire for enlightenment an obstacle to the guy who sat and ran after it for ten million years, if they which hunger after righteousness shall be filled? Would it have been more modest to quit trying so hard?

You have to come up with your own answer. But the bodhisattva strategy is to embrace the fabulous wealth that is here instead of desiring and holding on to a particular picture of what it should look like when it arrives.

The Buddha, in his sutra on the full awareness of breathing recommended this exercise: "Breathing in I observe the disappearance of desire. Breathing out I observe the disappearance of desire."

Thich Nhat Hanh's commentary on this explains: "We see that happiness does not lie in ideas about what we will realize in the future, and for that reason we are no longer attached to the objects of our desire that we thought would bring us future happiness."

Desire is attachment. Very sticky stuff.

Attachment is a primary cause of suffering in our lives, whether the suffering comes as disappointment, dissatisfaction, jealousy, regret, shame, impatience, or self-criticism. At its worst, Plato and the *I Ching* tell us, desire itself enslaves us. We cling to it furiously, we *want* to stay attached to what we picture bringing us future happiness, even at the expense of our own freedom. Desire for wealth, even desire for love, directly prevent us from embracing the love and wealth that exist for us in the present.

Proudly we cling to our desire, even the desire to see ourselves as "right." This is not the hunger for righteousness Jesus spoke of. This is clinging to our own chains.

And letting go can bring immediate liberation. The sages all say so. But we cover our ears with our chained hands. And you know why.

What Is Fabulous?

THE DICTIONARY SAYS, "resembling a fable, especially in incredible, marvelous, or exaggerated quality." In other words, something remarkable is exciting enough to remark on, but something fabulous is exciting enough to become part of a fable, "a legendary story of supernatural happenings." And the thing about these stories is we hear them as children, and the images we form in our child-minds then tend to stay with us all our lives.

So to become "fabulously wealthy" means to achieve or arrive at the wondrous circumstances some part of us has perhaps longed for since we formed our first pictures of personal success and wealth. The happy ending. The purpose of this booklet is to reprogram this as the picture of a happy beginning.

Become fabulously wealthy now, not later. No waiting. "Why wait any longer for the world to begin?" Bob Dylan once asked. The character speaking these words in his story-song was a lover, a supplicant. If we love ourselves, we could ask ourselves the same playful question: "Come live in a fabled mansion with me! I'll show it to you, dear one. We can get there by counting our blessings. And when we get there we can count our fabulous blessings together. Why wait any longer?"

Where Is Home?

IN 1999 THE INTERNET has changed the meaning of the word "home." "Home shopping" and "home banking" use the word to connote something you do on your computer instead of driving to a public building. Home is where the disc drive is. "Home" is also the first page of any website. Click on "home" and you theoretically get back to where you started from.

That world-traveling Vietnamese Zen poet Thich Nhat Hanh suggests another very modern (useful for world-travelers) interpretation of "home." He says to himself, while following his in-breaths and out-breaths mindfully:

I have arrived.
I am home.
In the here and in the now.

This exercise can be done on an airplane, or almost anywhere else a body finds its mind or vice versa. Breathing consciously reminds us that body and mind are connected; and every time a being remembers this, he or she arrives home. Returns to her- or him- self.

Where is home? Where one finds one's self. The throne of consciousness. Arrived at by meditation, or prayer, or any other sincere spiritual practice. Anyone can be a bodhisattva, an awakened being, and home is where you find yourself when you wake up.

The trouble with this definition of "home" is that if you're only at home in your awakened mind, how can you arrange to enjoy this wealth while you're out drinking with your friends?

So you get it... You can become fabulously wealthy at home in 30 minutes, but the catch is that when you're not home (not in your right, or righteous, mind) you're the same penniless bum you always were. Sorry about that.

This offer (this license) is not valid while the operator of the vehicle is unconscious.

"Fame or integrity: which is more important? Money or happiness: which is more valuable? Success or failure: which is more destructive?

"If you look to others for fulfillment, you will never truly be fulfilled. If your happiness depends on money, you will never be happy with yourself.

"Be content with what you have; rejoice in the way things are.

"When you realize there is nothing lacking, the whole world belongs to you."

— Lao-tzu, in the *Tao Te Ching*, Stephen Mitchell translation (1988)

"The whole world belongs to you." The kingdom of heaven. The pure land. Fabulous wealth.

Home is where you find yourself when you open your eyes or ears or heart... Wealth at home is different from wealth in the imagined (or nonexistent) future — more solid, more enjoyable, more spendable. But "at home" in this booklet's title also represents an implied promise that you the reader can learn how to become wealthy (by letting go...) without dashing off to a university or a monastery or a nunnery or some kind of workshop. You can learn this technique, start employing this strategy, at home. Right here. Right now. (No waiting.)

All this will happen just as soon as you're ready.

Bibliography:

Anthony, Carol K., *A Guide to the I Ching*, Anthony Publishing, 1980

Blyth, R. H., *Zen and Zen Classics, Volume Four, Mumonkan*, The Hokuseido Press, 1966

Chödrön, Pema, *Awakening Loving-Kindness*, Shambhala Publications, 1996

Fox, Emmet, *The Sermon on the Mount*, Harper & Row, Publishers, 1934

Mitchell, Stephen, translator, *Tao Te Ching*, Harper & Row, Publishers, 1988

Nhat Hanh, Thich, *Breathe! You Are Alive, The Sutra on the Full Awareness of Breathing* (translated from the Vietnamese by Annabel Laity), Parallax Press, 1996

Nhat Hanh, Thich, *Peace Is Every Step*, Bantam, 1991

Nhat Hanh, Thich, *Transformation & Healing, The Sutra on the Four Establishments of Mindfulness*, Parallax Press, 1990

Nhat Hanh, Thich, "Cultivating Our Bodhisattva Qualities" in *The Mindfulness Bell*, Fall 1998

Vonnegut, Kurt Jr., *God Bless You, Mr. Rosewater*, Holt, Rinehart and Winston, 1965

Wilhelm, Richard, translator, *The I Ching, or Book of Changes* (rendered into English by Cary F. Baynes), Princeton University Press/Bollingen Foundation, 1950

WORKBOOK SECTION

You may use these remaining pages of the book as a personal map to buried treasure, the wealth that is hidden in your life as it is right now.

This can be a private journal, or a playful game shared between friends or life-partners. The workbook pages are repeated several times, for the convenience of people who are sharing a copy of this book. When you fill out a page, write your name in an upper corner of the page, so you know who it is the whole world belongs to in this case.

Pages are also repeated because when one's wealth is truly fabulous, it takes a lot of entries to describe it and catalog it. And you may keep discovering new rooms full of treasure that you'd overlooked until now.

Two ways in which I am wealthy now:

1:

2:

Two more ways in which I am wealthy now:

1:

2:

Two more ways in which I am wealthy now:

1:

2:

Two more ways in which I am wealthy now:

1:

2:

What I appreciate about my earthly home:

1:

2:

What is fabulous to me:

1:

2:

My Blessings:

My Blessings:

Some opportunities for modesty and kindness:

Desires and attachments I might someday be able to let go of, just a little:

Two ways in which I am wealthy now:

1:

2:

Two more ways in which I am wealthy now:

1:

2:

Two more ways in which I am wealthy now:

1:

2:

Two more ways in which I am wealthy now:

1:

2:

What I appreciate about my earthly home:

1:

2:

What is fabulous to me:

1:

2:

My Blessings:

My Blessings:

Some opportunities for modesty and kindness:

**Desires and attachments I might
someday be able to let go of, just a little:**

Two ways in which I am wealthy now:

1:

2:

Two more ways in which I am wealthy now:

1:

2:

Two more ways in which I am wealthy now:

1:

2:

Two more ways in which I am wealthy now:

1:

2:

What I appreciate about my earthly home:

1:

2:

What is fabulous to me:

1:

2:

My Blessings:

My Blessings:

Some opportunities for modesty and kindness:

Desires and attachments I might someday be able to let go of, just a little:

BOOKS BY PAUL WILLIAMS:

Practical philosophy:

Das Energi
Remember Your Essence
Fear of Truth (Energi Inscriptions)
Waking Up Together
The Book of Houses (with astrologer Robert Cole)
Coming
Nation of Lawyers
Common Sense
How to Become Fabulously Wealthy at Home in 30 Minutes

Hippie memoirs:

Time Between
Apple Bay or Life on the Planet
Heart of Gold

Collections:

Pushing Upward
Right to Pass and Other True Stories

Music:

Performing Artist, The Music of Bob Dylan, Volumes I & II
Brian Wilson & the Beach Boys — How Deep Is the Ocean?
Neil Young — Love to Burn
Rock and Roll: The 100 Best Singles
Watching the River Flow: Observations on Bob Dylan's Art-in-Progress 1966-1995
The Map — Rediscovering Rock and Roll
Outlaw Blues
Back to the Miracle Factory

Other arts:

The 20th Century's Greatest Hits
Only Apparently Real: The World of Philip K. Dick

Edited by Paul Williams:

The International Bill of Human Rights
The Complete Stories of Theodore Sturgeon
(magazines: *Crawdaddy!* *The PKD Society Newsletter*)

ALL in print. For a catalog or ordering information, contact:
Entwhistle Books, Box 232517 Encinitas CA 92023 USA
www.cdaddy.com (look for **Entwhistle Books** button)
phone or fax: 760-753-1815   email: EB@cdaddy.com

www.ingramcontent.com/pod-product-compliance
Lightning Source LLC
Chambersburg PA
CBHW021203020426
42331CB00003B/182